PREPARE THE WAY

Advent and Christmas Bible Stories for Kids

JARED DEES

Scripture texts in this work are based on the New Revised Standard Version Bible, copyright © 1989 the Division of Christian Education of the National Council of the Churches of Christ in the United States of America. Used by permission. All rights reserved.

———————————————

For more information, visit jareddees.com.

Paperback: ISBN 978-1-954135-00-0
eBook: ISBN 978-1-954135-01-7

First Edition

CONTENTS

INTRODUCTION

Christmastime is a wonderful time of year. Most kids —and grown-ups!—consider Christmas to be their favorite season. Why? Because we get presents, of course! On Christmas we celebrate the greatest gift in the world: the birth of our Lord Jesus Christ. We prepare our lives and hearts to celebrate God becoming man.

In the Church we celebrate an entire season of preparation in the four weeks leading up to Christmas. We call this season of preparation Advent. Advent is a word that means "to come." It is a season to remind ourselves of what we will celebrate on Christmas: Jesus Christ, the Son of God, came into the world and became one of us.

But the weeks leading up to Christmas are often the most stressful time of the year, especially for parents. The season of Advent reminds us of what is most important as we prepare for Christmas. Jesus Christ is God's greatest gift to the world.

Advent is also a season to remember that Jesus Christ will come back. Jesus died, rose from the dead, and ascended to heaven, where he is now with the Father. He told his disciples to be ready for his return at any moment. So, in addition to remembering the gift of Jesus coming into the world 2,000 years ago, we prepare the way for Jesus to come back into the world at any time.

This book is a collection of the Bible stories we often hear during the seasons of Advent and Christmas. The stories will help us to prepare for celebrating the birth of Christ, and they will help us prepare for his return.

As the saying goes, "Jesus is the reason for the season," but who is Jesus Christ? Who is the one that we prepare to meet at Christmas?

During Advent and Christmas, we hear and reflect on so many names and titles for the Lord:

He is the promised **Messiah**, the "Anointed One" and king of Israel, though he doesn't have a throne in this world.

He is **Emmanuel**, which means "God is with us."

He is **Jesus**, which means "God saves."

He is the **Son of Man**, who will return to judge the nations.

He is the **Son of God**, who came into the world and became one of us.

As you read these stories, alone or together as a family, think about the ways you can stay focused on what matters most during this season. How can you prepare the way for his presence in the world and in your hearts? Read these stories to find out.

"Prepare the way of the Lord, make his paths straight."

Matthew 3:3 (see also Isaiah 40:3)

ADVENT: THE SECOND COMING

We begin the season of Advent with an ending. At the end of the world, Jesus Christ will come back. We don't know when. It could be at any time, and Jesus warned us to be ready.

The following Advent stories help us to prepare the way for the Lord to return.

BE WATCHFUL AND ALERT

Matthew 24:45–51; Mark 13:34–37; Luke 12:35–48

Jesus told his disciples that he would return after his death and ascension into heaven. To help them prepare for his return, he told them a parable to warn them how to be ready.

As you read this story, pay attention to the reasons the servants had such a hard time waiting for their master to return.

Jesus gathered his disciples together to tell them about his return. They came together to listen to his words.

He told them a group of servants were waiting late into the night for their master to return from a wedding. He had asked them to stay awake and wait for his return at the door.

It became late and dark. They kept the lamps of the house lit. They stood by the gate, waiting for him to arrive so that they could open it as soon as he knocked.

It was hard to wait. They didn't know what time he would come back. He could arrive in the evening, or at midnight, or by sunrise the next day. They had no idea.

No matter how tired they felt or how bored they got, they stayed awake and ready for him to come back.

The master returned very late into the night, and the tired servants welcomed him home. Then he surprised them.

He brought them to the dining room and invited them to sit and eat. The master went into the kitchen and prepared a meal for them. He served the servants himself.

Jesus ended the story and said to his disciples, "Blessed is the servant whom the master will find at work when he arrives. Be watchful and alert, for you do not know when the Son of Man will come. He will come at an unexpected hour."

REFLECTION QUESTIONS

Why was it so difficult for the servants to wait for their master to return?

If Jesus returned today, would you be ready?

What can you do today to prepare for Jesus Christ's return?

THE COMING OF THE SON OF MAN

Matthew 24:29–31; Mark 13:24–27; Luke 21:25–28, 34–36

Jesus said he would return. He also described what his disciples should expect to experience before his return.

As you read this story, pay attention to the things we can expect to see before Jesus comes back to the world.

Jesus told his disciples, "There will be many signs upon my return. The sun and the moon will be darkened. The stars will fall from the sky. The earth will be in distress. The sea will roar and there will be great waves.

"People will be afraid of what is coming upon the world. The powers of the heavens will be shaken.

"Then the people will see the Son of Man coming in a cloud with great power and glory. He will send out his angels with a loud trumpet call, and they will gather the elect from all the ends of the earth.

"Be on guard not to let the worries of this life weigh your heart down. Do not be distracted by temptations. Do not let my return come upon you unexpectedly like a trap. Watch, therefore; you do not know the day nor the hour.

"Be alert at all times. Pray that you will have the strength to escape all these things and be ready to stand before the Son of Man."

REFLECTION QUESTIONS

What signs will we experience before Jesus's return?

What are some of the worries of this life that weigh your heart down?

Would you be ready for Jesus to return today? Why or why not?

THE SHEEP AND THE GOATS

Matthew 25:31–46

Jesus told his disciples about the final judgment so that he could teach them about how they should live their lives before he came back. His message still applies today to us who await his return.

As you read this story, pay attention to the expectations Jesus the king has for his people.

When the Son of Man comes in glory, you will see angels with him and he will sit on a great throne.

All the people of the world will be gathered together before him. Then he will separate everyone into two groups just as a shepherd separates the sheep from the goats.

He will put the sheep on his right side and the goats on his left. The king will turn to the people on his right and say, "Come, you are blessed by my Father. The kingdom has been prepared for you since the beginning of time. I was hungry and you gave me food. I was thirsty and you gave me a drink. I was a stranger, yet you welcomed me like you knew me. I needed clothes and you gave them to me. I was sick and you helped me get well. I was in jail and you visited me."

The people on the right will be confused. "Lord, when did we do these things for you?" they will ask.

The king will answer them, "Just as you did for the least in my family, you did for me."

Then the king will turn to the people on his left and say, "You are cursed. Depart from me into the eternal fire prepared for the devil and his demons. I was hungry and you did not feed me. I was thirsty and you gave me no drink. I was a stranger and you sent me away. I needed clothing and you gave me no clothes. I was sick and you let me suffer. I was in prison and you never came to see me."

These people will be confused as well. They will say, "Lord, when did we not take care of you?"

The king will reply, "Just as you did not do for the lowest people in the world, you did not do for me."

These people will go to eternal punishment, while the others will join the king in eternal life.

REFLECTION QUESTIONS

Why were some people welcomed into the kingdom for eternal life and others sent into eternal punishment?

How can you do each of the things Jesus expects of his disciples? How can you give food, drink, and clothing? How can you welcome strangers, help the sick, and comfort people in jail?

Have you ever seen someone who is homeless? What can you do to help them?

ADVENT: THE PROMISED MESSIAH

When Jesus was born, his people were waiting for a king to come to Israel whose kingdom would last forever. They called this king the Messiah, which means the "Anointed One." Christ isn't Jesus's last name. Christ is a title that means Messiah. Jesus Christ is Jesus, the Anointed One, who God promised would come to rule his people.

The following Advent stories are from the Old Testament, but they talk about Jesus Christ who would come into the world.

SAMUEL ANOINTS DAVID AS KING

1 Samuel 16:1–13

Jesus Christ was born King of the Jews. He was descended from King David, who was a most unlikely king. This is the story of how Jesus's ancestor David became the king of Israel.

As you read this story, pay attention to the reasons that the Lord withheld his blessing from the older sons of Jesse and anointed David as king.

God was disappointed in Saul, the king of Israel. He told the prophet Samuel to anoint another person as king.

The Lord said to the prophet, "Fill your horn with oil. Go to Bethlehem, where you will find a man named Jesse. I have provided for myself a king from among his sons."

So Samuel traveled to Bethlehem and invited Jesse and his sons to a blessing ceremony. The father and his boys joined Samuel, as he requested.

First, Jesse brought forth his oldest son, Eliab.

Samuel saw the young man and thought to himself, "Surely this is the one the Lord wants me to anoint as king."

But the Lord said to Samuel, "Do not look on his appearance or on his height, because I have rejected him; for the Lord does not see as humans see. Humans look on the outward appearance, but the Lord looks on the heart."

Jesse called another son up to bring before Samuel, but the Lord said to him, "Neither has the Lord chosen this one."

Jesse brought seven of his sons before Samuel, but the Lord said that none of them were his chosen one.

Finally, Samuel said to Jesse, "Are all your sons here?"

Jesse said, "No, there is one more, my youngest son, David. He is out in the fields, keeping watch over the sheep."

"Send for him and bring him to me," the prophet instructed.

Jesse sent for David, who arrived soon afterward. He had rosy cheeks and beautiful eyes. He was very handsome.

Suddenly, the Lord said to Samuel, "Rise, and anoint him; for this is the one."

The prophet Samuel took the horn of oil and anointed the youngest son in the presence of all his older brothers. The spirit of the Lord came mightily upon David from that day forward. He was to become the king of Israel.

REFLECTION QUESTIONS

Why did the Lord wish to bless and anoint David and not one of his older brothers as king?

Why do you think it is so difficult to look on the heart of other people rather than their outward appearance?

In what ways can you become humble so that God can bless you?

GOD'S PROMISE TO DAVID

2 Samuel 7

When Jesus was born, God's people were waiting for the Messiah to come and sit on the throne of David. They believed in a promise God had made to King David that he would establish his kingdom forever. This is the story of that promise.

As you read this story, pay attention to the ways the Lord describes David's descendant, Jesus Christ.

David had won many great battles and entered into his new capital city of Jerusalem. He was just getting settled into his palace when he summoned the prophet Nathan.

He said to the prophet, "Here I am living in a great palace, yet there is no house here for God. Should I build him a temple?"

At first Nathan agreed that the king should build the temple, but that night, God spoke to the prophet.

"Go and tell David my servant that I have never dwelt in a house since the day I brought Israel up out of Egypt. I long wandered with the people and never asked for a temple," God told him.

This answered David's question about the temple, but then the Lord added another message. The Lord promised to establish an everlasting house for David and his descendants. He wasn't just talking about a building. He wanted to tell David about a descendant who would rule forever.

The prophet Nathan returned to the king and proclaimed, "Thus says the Lord of hosts: You were a shepherd, but I turned you into the ruler of Israel. I was with you wherever you went, and I will make your name as great as the greatest ones on earth.

"Your son will build me a temple, but in you and your descendants I will make a house and a throne that will last forever. I will raise up an offspring after you, and I will establish his kingdom. I will be a father to him, and he shall be a son to me. Your house and your kingdom will last forever."

Then King David knelt down in prayer to praise God, saying, "Who am I, Lord God, that you have brought me so far? You have made such a great promise. You are great, O Lord God, and there is no one like you."

Then King David praised God for the people of Israel, saying, "Who is like your people? Is there another nation on earth whose God went to redeem them and make a name for himself? You establish your people forever for yourself, and you, O Lord, became their God."

Then, finally, King David asked for God's blessing, saying, "As for the word you have spoken about your servant and this kingdom, please do as you have promised. Your name will be magnified forever as the Lord God over Israel. O Lord God, you are God, and your words are true. You have promised this good thing to your servant. Bless this house and your servant so that the kingdom may continue forever before you. With your blessing, may the house of King David be blessed forever!"

REFLECTION QUESTIONS

In what ways do you think the Lord's promise referred to Jesus Christ?

How do you look to Jesus Christ as your king today?

King David offered a prayer of praise to God. What praise can you give to God for the work he has done in your life this year?

THE ROOT OF JESSE

Isaiah 11:1–10

In addition to an Advent wreath, the Jesse Tree is a common way to count the days leading up to Christmas. Each day, we remember an ancestor of Jesus, leading all the way back to Jesse, the father of King David. This story is the prophet Isaiah's description of what Jesus, the descendant of Jesse and David, will do for the world.

As you read this story, pay attention to what the world will be like when the Messiah comes.

There will be a day when a man is born as a descendant of King David. He will be like a plant growing out of the roots of a tree stump. That stump is Jesse, the father of King David.

From the roots of that stump will grow a blossoming flower, a man who will do many great things.

Upon him the Holy Spirit will rest. He will receive a Spirit of wisdom and understanding, counsel and strength, knowledge, and fear of the Lord.

He will judge with righteousness. He will bring justice for the poor and meek of the world. He will be an example for all of faithfulness and righteousness.

When he comes, it will be as if a wolf lives with the lambs rather than eating them. A lion will lie down with the cows and not kill them. Cows and bears will graze the fields. Lions will eat straw instead of meat. A little child will lead them all.

A baby will play safely by the hole of a snake. A child will place his hand in the hole and take it out unbitten.

It will be a time of great peace in the world. No harm will come to those on the holy mountain of the Lord. The entire world will be filled with the knowledge of the Lord, just like the waters of the sea.

On the day that he will come, a signal will be raised for all the nations of the world. Even the Gentiles, who are not from the people of Israel, will seek him out, and his house will be glorious.

REFLECTION QUESTIONS

What will the world be like when the Messiah comes?

How has Jesus brought peace into your heart and life?

How are you like a signal to the world showing the peace that God can give?

THE PROMISE OF EMMANUEL

Isaiah 7

One of the most important prophecies about the Messiah came from the prophet Isaiah to the king of Judah. At that time, God's people were divided into two kingdoms: Israel in the north and Judah in the south. The rulers of the kingdoms did not get along, and many of their kings struggled to stay faithful to God.

As you read this story, pay attention to the reasons why Ahaz reaches out for the help of the Assyrians instead of God.

It was a difficult time for the people of Judah when Ahaz became the king. There were many foreign kingdoms with great power that were much stronger than God's people, and even the northern kingdom of Israel opposed Judah.

King Ahaz sat on his throne in Jerusalem, filled with worry. The Assyrians in the north were planning to invade. The kings of Israel and Aram wanted to attack

Ahaz's kingdom to get their armies and supplies before the Assyrians invaded.

Ahaz didn't know whose side he should be on. He didn't know where to get help to withstand his enemies.

Then the Lord sent the prophet Isaiah to meet with King Ahaz. Isaiah met him on the road outside of Jerusalem.

The prophet said to the king, "Take care and remain calm. Be quiet and do not fear. Do not let your heart be troubled because of Aram and Israel. They have planned evil against you, but their plans will fail."

The king was amazed, but he wondered what this meant.

The prophet continued, "It shall not stand, and it shall not come to pass. These enemies of yours will fall. But if you do not stand firm in faith, you shall not stand at all."

"So what shall I do then?" asked the king.

"Ask for a sign from the Lord," Isaiah responded.

"I will not ask. I will not put the Lord to the test," replied the king.

Then the prophet spoke, saying, "Hear then, O house of David! The Lord himself will give you a sign. You will see a young woman, pregnant and about to bear a son. She will name him Emmanuel."

He continued, "These two enemies that plot against you will be long gone. The Lord will bring to your descendants such days as have not been in a very long time."

But Ahaz did not listen. He did not trust in the Lord. He asked for the help of the mighty Assyrians to defeat the northern kingdom of Israel and the kingdom of Aram. Ahaz was responsible for the loss of many of God's people, who were taken away from Israel to Assyria.

When King Ahaz died, his son Hezekiah took the throne. Hezekiah listened to the prophet Isaiah and trusted in the Lord, who protected him from the Assyrians when they betrayed Judah and tried to conquer their kingdom.

But not all kings remained loyal to the Lord. After a few generations, the mighty Babylonians came and conquered the kingdom of Judah. All seemed to be lost until many years later, when an angel appeared to a young woman in Galilee named Mary, who bore a son.

REFLECTION QUESTIONS

Why did King Ahaz reach out to the Assyrians for help?

Have you ever had a hard time trusting in God? Why was it so hard?

Emmanuel means "God is with us." What reminds you that God is with you?

ADVENT: JOHN THE BAPTIST

The prophet Isaiah said that a voice would cry out in the wilderness to prepare the way for the coming of the Messiah. John the Baptist was that voice; he was sent to help people prepare for the coming of the Lord. For that reason, John is a model for us to meditate on during the season of Advent.

THE BIRTH OF JOHN THE BAPTIST

Luke 1:5–25, 57–80

The story of the birth of John the Baptist is a reminder to us to trust in God no matter how unbelievable his plans might be. John's parents, Zechariah and Elizabeth, thought they were too old to have children, yet God planned to bless them with a son.

As you read this story, pay attention to the way the angel describes what John the Baptist will become.

Zechariah was a priest. His wife's name was Elizabeth. They were good and holy people. They followed the commandments and set a great example for the people that knew them. Sadly, however, they were unable to have any children. They prayed for a child as a gift from God.

Zechariah was working as a priest in the temple one day while people were praying outside. He offered incense to the Lord, and suddenly, an angel appeared to him.

"Do not be afraid, Zechariah, for your prayers have been heard. Your wife, Elizabeth, will have a son, and you will name him John," said the angel.

Zechariah was in shock, both at the sight of the angel and at the angel's words.

"You will be filled with joy, and many others will rejoice in the birth of your son. He will be filled with the Holy Spirit and turn many people back to the Lord their God. He will prepare the way for the Lord," the angel continued.

But Zechariah was in disbelief. "How can I know this is true? I am an old man, and my wife is old, too."

"I am Gabriel. I stand in the presence of God, who sent me to you to bring this good news. But since you did not believe in my words, you will become unable to speak until the birth of your son," said the angel Gabriel.

Outside, the people started to worry about Zechariah. He had been in the Temple a long time. When he finally came out, they saw that he could not speak. They realized he must have had some kind of vision.

He returned home, and soon his wife became pregnant. "Look what the Lord has done for me," she said excitedly to Zechariah. "He has looked upon me with his favor and blessed me."

Many months later, Elizabeth gave birth to a son. Her neighbors and relatives rejoiced with her, knowing that

God had blessed her in her old age. They suggested that the boy be named Zechariah after his father.

"No," she said. "We will name him John."

"But no one in your family is named John. Why would you name him that?" they said.

Zechariah was still unable to speak because he had doubted the angel's words in the Temple. When the people came to him to ask about the name of the child, he wrote on a tablet, "His name is John."

Suddenly, he was able to speak again. He immediately praised God not only for his answered prayer but for God's great plan for his son, who would become known as John the Baptist.

REFLECTION QUESTIONS

What did the angel say John the Baptist would do?

When have you put your trust in God to do something that seemed impossible?

What answered prayers can you praise God for giving to you?

THE PREACHING OF JOHN THE BAPTIST

Matthew 3:1–11; Mark 1:2–8; Luke 3:1–16; John 1:19–27

John the Baptist was the best known preacher in all of Judea. He preached an important message to help prepare the way of the Lord.

As you read this story, pay attention to the message John the Baptist shared with his disciples in the wilderness.

A very inspiring man lived in the wilderness of Judea, repeating to all who came to listen to him, "Repent, for the kingdom of heaven is near!" His name was John the Baptist.

John the Baptist was a unique person. He owned nothing. He wore uncomfortable camel's hair and a leather belt. He fasted every day, eating only wild honey and bugs called locusts.

The rumors spread about him. Many wondered if he was the Messiah who the prophets predicted would return someday for the salvation of Israel.

But the prophet Isaiah had said that there would be a voice in the wilderness before the Messiah returned, crying out, "Prepare the way of the Lord, make his paths straight!"

When a few priests came to ask John who he was, he replied, "I am not the Messiah. I am the voice of one crying out in the wilderness, 'Make straight the way of the Lord.'"

John told the people who came to listen to him to change their ways and repent. Those who wished to change and receive forgiveness from God joined John at the Jordan River. He took them down into the river and washed them, saying, "I baptize you with water for repentance and forgiveness of sins, but one who is more powerful than I is coming after me. I am not worthy to untie his sandals. I baptize you with water, but he will baptize you with the Holy Spirit."

The people wondered who this might be. Surely John the Baptist was preparing them for the coming of the Messiah. None of them realized it at the time, but a local man named Jesus of Nazareth was coming to meet John in the wilderness, too.

REFLECTION QUESTIONS

What message did John the Baptist preach?

How can you change your ways, and what sins do you need God to forgive today?

How can you prepare the way for Jesus to be present in your life?

CHRISTMAS STORIES

The following stories describe the events before, during, and after the birth of Christ. They tell the story of the Holy Family of Joseph, Mary, and Jesus and what Mary and Joseph had to go through to bring the child into the world. Then, we conclude the series of Christmas stories with the story of a new birth we share in with Jesus: his baptism.

THE ANNUNCIATION

Luke 1:26–38

A young woman named Mary lived in Galilee. She was engaged to marry a man named Joseph. An angel appeared to Mary to announce the birth of her son, and her reaction provides for us a wonderful example of faith.

As you read this story, pay attention to the way the Virgin Mary responds to the words of the angel Gabriel.

The angel Gabriel appeared to the Virgin Mary, saying, "Hail, favored one! The Lord is with you."

Mary was confused by the angel's words and wondered what he meant by this.

The angel said to her, "Do not be afraid, Mary, for you have found favor with God. Behold, you will conceive in your womb and bear a son, and you will name him Jesus. He will be great and will be called the Son of the Most High. He will be a king, and his kingdom will have no end."

Mary said to the angel, "How can this be, since I am still unmarried and a virgin?"

The angel replied, "The Holy Spirit will come upon you, and the power of the Most High will overshadow you. The child to be born will be holy. He will be called Son of God."

As if to erase any other doubt, the angel continued, "Your cousin Elizabeth has also conceived a son in her old age. She is already six months pregnant. For nothing will be impossible with God."

Mary responded with an act of humble faith in God's will. She said, "Behold, I am the handmaid of the Lord. May it be done to me according to your word."

It was an awesome responsibility, and both Mary and Joseph placed their trust in the Lord to give them the strength to do his will.

REFLECTION QUESTIONS

How did Mary react to the words of the angel?

In what ways can we become handmaids (or servants) of the Lord?

In what areas of your life do you need to trust in God more and let things be done according to his will and not yours?

THE VISITATION

Luke 1:39-56

The Virgin Mary didn't have to go through pregnancy alone. Her cousin Elizabeth was also pregnant, with John the Baptist. From Mary's visit with her cousin, we learn more about her calling and the significance of her unborn son.

As you read this story, pay attention to the things the Virgin Mary says about herself and her son in her prayer of praise.

The angel Gabriel told Mary that her cousin Elizabeth, who everyone thought was unable to have children, was six months pregnant. Mary set out quickly to visit her cousin in the hill country.

Mary arrived at her cousin's house and knocked at the door. When Elizabeth heard Mary, her unborn child leaped in her womb.

Elizabeth was filled with the Holy Spirit and said, "Blessed are you among women, and blessed is the fruit of your womb. How can it be that the mother of my Lord comes to me? Blessed is she who believed that there would be fulfillment of what was spoken to her by the Lord!"

Mary was moved by her cousin's words. She offered up her own prayer of praise, saying, "My soul magnifies the Lord, and my spirit rejoices in God my Savior, for he has looked with favor on the lowliness of his servant. Surely, from now on, all generations will call me blessed; for the Mighty One has done great things for me, and holy is his name."

Then she continued her prayer of praise for all the things her son would do for the world, saying, "The Lord's mercy is for those who fear him. He separates the proud with their selfish thoughts. He brings down the powerful leaders and lifts up the lowly, filling the hungry with good things and sending the rich away empty."

Finally, speaking of God's people, she proclaimed, "The Lord has helped Israel, remembering his mercy according to the promise he made to Abraham and our ancestors and their descendants forever."

Mary remained with her cousin Elizabeth for three months and then returned home.

REFLECTION QUESTIONS

What did Mary say about herself and her son in her prayer of praise to God?

What great things has God done for you, and what can you say in praise of his gifts to you?

How can you become a lowly servant of God in the way you live your life today?

JOSEPH'S ANNUNCIATION

Matthew 1:18–25

God sent the angel Gabriel to Mary, but he also sent an angel to Joseph to ensure that Jesus would be protected as a child.

As you read this story, pay attention to the way Joseph responds to the angel of God's commands.

Joseph and Mary were engaged to be married. To Joseph's surprise, Mary became pregnant. Joseph knew this was impossible. They weren't married yet.

Mary told Joseph about the experience she'd had with the angel Gabriel and how the child came from the Holy Spirit.

Joseph was afraid of what people might think of them. He decided that quietly ending their engagement might be best for her and the child.

But before he could share the plans with Mary, an angel of the Lord appeared to him in a dream.

The angel said, "Joseph, son of David, do not be afraid to take Mary as your wife. The child is from the Holy Spirit. She will have a son, and you will name him Jesus, which means 'God saves.' He will save his people from their sins."

Joseph was a righteous man. He knew the scriptures well. He remembered the words of the prophet Isaiah:

"Look, a virgin shall conceive and bear a son, and they shall name him Emmanuel," which Joseph knew to mean "God is with us."

Then the angel disappeared and Joseph woke up. He did exactly as the angel told him to do. Joseph and Mary became husband and wife. Later, when the child was born, they named him Jesus, just as the angel had asked him to do.

REFLECTION QUESTIONS

What did the angel tell Joseph to do?

What do the names Jesus and Emmanuel mean?

How does God give you the courage to do what is right?

When do you feel that God is with you the most?

NO ROOM IN THE INN

Luke 2:1–7

The prophets in the Old Testament said that the Messiah would be born in Bethlehem, a city of David, but Mary and Joseph lived in Nazareth. Here is the story of how Jesus came to be born in Bethlehem, near the capital city of Jerusalem.

As you read this story, pay attention to the humble beginnings of the life of the Lord Jesus Christ.

Emperor Augustus ruled over all the lands within the Roman Empire, including Israel. There were many people in the empire. The emperor wanted to know how many people he ruled over and where they came from.

He sent out a decree from Rome that everyone should briefly return to their hometown to be registered and counted.

Joseph and Mary lived in Nazareth, but Joseph's family was from a town called Bethlehem. Bethlehem was a place where the descendants of King David lived. David was one of Joseph's ancestors.

Because of the decree, Joseph and Mary had to leave Nazareth and head to Bethlehem. But Mary was already nine months pregnant. Her son could be born at any moment.

They arrived in Bethlehem and went looking for a place to stay. The city was very crowded. It was so crowded that not a single inn had a room for them.

One innkeeper welcomed them. He didn't have a room for them, but he made a place for them in a stable in the farm behind the inn.

There would be no bed for Mary to lay her son in once he was born. Instead, there was a manger, which was used to hold food for the animals in the stable.

The time came for Mary to give birth. There in the stable, the King of kings was born into the world. There was no palace and no throne. This was the humble beginning of the extraordinary life of the Lord. They named him Jesus, which means "God saves," just as an angel had instructed them. Mary wrapped him in swaddling clothes and laid him in the manger.

REFLECTION QUESTIONS

Why was Jesus born in Bethlehem instead of Nazareth?

Have you ever helped someone even when it felt hard or impossible?

Instead of demanding a room, Joseph and Mary humbly accepted a stable for Jesus to be born in. How can you accept disappointment with grace and humility like them?

THE VISIT FROM THE SHEPHERDS

Luke 2:8–20

The very first people to meet the Lord Jesus Christ, newborn King of the Jews, were simple shepherds, not great leaders. It was a miraculous event, and yet some of the poorest people in the land were the first to know about it.

As you read this story, pay attention to the message that the angel brings to the shepherds near Bethlehem.

Not far from Bethlehem, where Jesus had been born, there were shepherds in a field watching over their sheep. Suddenly, an angel of the Lord appeared to them in glory. The shepherds were struck with fear.

"Do not be afraid," the angel said to them. "Behold, I bring you good news of great joy for all the world. To you this day is born in Bethlehem a Savior, who is the Messiah, the Lord. You will find him wrapped in swaddling clothes and lying in a manger."

Then the shepherds saw many angels appear, praising God, saying, "Glory to God in the highest, and on earth, peace to those on whom his favor rests!"

The angels left them, and the shepherds went as fast as they could to find Mary and Joseph and the baby lying in the manger. The shepherds told the new parents all that the angels had said about the child. Mary and Joseph were amazed.

Mary would treasure all that she heard and think deeply about the shepherds' words in her heart in the years to come. The shepherds went away glorifying and praising God for all that they had seen and heard. As the angel said, this is good news for the whole world. There were many people that needed to hear this message of hope.

REFLECTION QUESTIONS

What message did the angel bring to the shepherds?

In what ways does Jesus bring peace into our world today?

How can we, like Mary, think deeply about this and other stories from the Bible?

THE VISIT OF THE THREE WISE MEN

Matthew 2:1–12

Jesus Christ was the Messiah. He was the King of the Jews, yet his spiritual kingdom would extend beyond Israel. The three wise men were foreigners, but they came from their country to find the prophesied king.

As you read this story, pay attention to the reason the wise men from the east come to find Jesus.

East of Israel, in another country, three wise men saw a unique star rising up into the sky. These three men left their homes to follow the star, for they knew it meant a new king was born in Israel.

The men traveled to Jerusalem and asked to meet with King Herod, who was the appointed king of the Jews.

"Where is the child who has been born King of the Jews?" they asked him.

Herod was quite upset about the question. He was already the king of the Jews. "Why do you ask this?" he said to them.

"We saw a star rising up into the sky, so we came to pay our respects to him," they said.

King Herod dismissed the wise men and called for his chief priests and scribes to ask about the star. He was worried someone would come to take away his power. He knew the scriptures told of a Messiah that would be born King of the Jews.

"Where is the Messiah supposed to be born?" he asked them.

"Why, in Bethlehem of Judea, of course. This was told to us through the prophet Micah: 'But you, O Bethlehem, from you shall come forth for me one who is to rule in Israel, whose origin is from of old, from ancient days," they said.

Herod called for the wise men to return. He asked them more questions about the star, and his fear grew.

"Go and find the child. When you find him, come back and tell me where he is, so I can go and show my respect to him, too," he said to them, but secretly he wished to learn the whereabouts of the child so he could kill him.

The king released them, and they followed the star to the small town of Bethlehem. When they saw they were at the place where the star stopped, they were filled with joy.

They saw Mary and Joseph with the child. Mary welcomed them, and they each knelt down and bowed their heads before the newborn king.

The wise men raised their heads and greeted Mary. They opened three gifts that they had brought for the child. The gifts were fit for a king. They'd brought gold, frankincense, and myrrh.

They stayed only a little while. That night, they had a dream that warned them not to return to King Herod. Instead, they returned home to their country by another road.

REFLECTION QUESTIONS

Why did the wise men come to find Jesus?

Why was Herod so afraid of the news from the wise men?

How can you pay respect to Jesus?

What gifts can you give to God with your life?

THE PRESENTATION IN THE TEMPLE

Luke 2:22–39

Mary and Joseph were Jewish. They raised Jesus in the Jewish customs from his earliest days, including visits to the Temple in Jerusalem.

As you read this story, pay attention to the message Simeon and Anna share about what Jesus will do for the world.

Before Mary and Joseph returned to their home in Nazareth, they brought the baby Jesus to the temple. This was to fulfill a religious custom from the Old Testament to dedicate firstborn sons as holy to the Lord.

As they arrived at the Temple, a man named Simeon came running up to them. They could see in his eyes great joy at the sight of the child.

He took him in his arms and praised God, saying, "Master, now you can send your servant away in peace, for my eyes have seen your salvation, which you have prepared for all people. He will be a light for the Gentiles who do not yet believe in you today and glory for your people of Israel."

Joseph and Mary were amazed by what Simeon said about their son.

Simeon blessed them and returned the child to Mary's arms. He said to her, "This child has an important destiny. Some will rise and some will fall before him. The hidden thoughts of many hearts will be revealed, and a sword will pierce your heart, too."

Then Simeon left and another person came up to them. It was a prophetess named Anna. She was very old and lonely. Her husband had died seven years earlier. She spent every moment of her day praying in the Temple and worshipping God.

When she saw the baby Jesus, she began to praise God and speak about the child to all who would listen to her. She told them about the redemption that this infant would bring to the city of Jerusalem and all of God's people.

Mary and Joseph finished their religious duty by making a sacrifice of purification for their son in the Temple. As they did, they wondered what was in store for him.

REFLECTION QUESTIONS

What did Simeon and Anna say that Jesus would do?

Why do you think this message about Jesus is so important today?

Simeon and Anna had waited a long time to meet Jesus. When have you had to wait to be with the Lord?

THE ESCAPE TO EGYPT

Matthew 2:13–23

King Herod was an evil ruler in Israel. He was not a descendant of King David and therefore not the rightful ruler. He feared the return of the Messiah. He was afraid to lose his power, and he would stop at nothing to keep it.

As you read this story, pay attention to the loyalty and obedience Joseph showed to God's message through the angel.

After Jesus was born in Bethlehem, Joseph and Mary prepared to return home to Nazareth. Before they returned, the angel of the Lord appeared to Joseph in a dream again.

The angel said, "Get up! Take the child and his mother to Egypt. Remain there until you hear from me again. King Herod will search for the child and try to kill him."

Joseph woke up in the middle of the night. There was no time to waste. He woke Mary, and they took Jesus and left immediately for Egypt.

Meanwhile, King Herod was furious. The three wise men had never returned to tell him where the Messiah was born. He ordered his soldiers to find and kill all of the infant children in and around Bethlehem.

The people of Bethlehem mourned the loss of the children by the hand of the evil King Herod. It was devastating and evil. They wished for a good king that would bring them freedom and salvation. They wished that the Messiah would return as the rightful king.

That king was Jesus. The Messiah remained in Egypt with Mary and Joseph until it was safe to return home.

Years passed, and Herod finally died. The angel of the Lord appeared to Joseph in a dream once more, saying, "Get up! Take the child and his mother back to the land of Israel."

Joseph, Mary, and Jesus left Egypt and went to Judea to their home in the town of Nazareth.

REFLECTION QUESTIONS

Why might it have been hard for Joseph to take his family to Egypt according to the angel's command?

Have you ever moved from one home to another, as Jesus, Mary, and Joseph did? What was that experience like?

What makes a leader good rather than evil?

THE BAPTISM OF JESUS

Matthew 3:13–17; Mark 1:9–11; Luke 3:21–22

We conclude this collection of Advent and Christmas Bible stories at the baptism of the Lord. On Christmas, we celebrate the birth of Jesus. In baptism, we celebrate a rebirth with Christ. We are born into the family of God.

As you read this story, pay attention to the way Jesus is described after he emerges from the waters of his baptism.

As John the Baptist became famous and gathered many followers in the wilderness, no one had heard of a man named Jesus from Nazareth.

But one day Jesus went out into the wilderness to visit John.

John was amazed. "I should be baptized by you, and yet you come to me?" he asked.

"Let it be for now. It is proper for us to fulfill all righteousness," Jesus replied.

John didn't object anymore. Jesus walked into the water of the Jordan River, and John baptized him there.

Jesus emerged from the water, and the clouds opened up. The sun shone bright and the Holy Spirit came down from heaven like a dove and rested on Jesus.

Then a voice came from heaven, saying, "This is my Beloved Son, with whom I am well pleased."

REFLECTION QUESTIONS

How did God identify Jesus after his baptism?

How does God love us like a father? How can we love him as his children?

How have you experienced God as the Father, Son, and Holy Spirit in your life?

ABOUT BIBLE BREAKS

The Bible Breaks stories for kids help families and faith formation groups set aside a few minutes during the day to read and reflect on the Word of God. Each short and simple story is written to help teach children the most important lessons of the Christian life from sacred Scripture.

Learn more at jareddees.com/biblebreaks

ALSO BY JARED DEES

Jared Dees is the author of numerous books, including a short story collection titled *Beatitales: 80 Fables about the Beatitudes for Children*.

Download a collection of these stories at jareddees.com/beatitales.

BOOKS BY JARED DEES

31 Days to Becoming a Better Religious Educator

To Heal, Proclaim, and Teach

Praying the Angelus

Christ in the Classroom

Beatitales

Tales of the Ten Commandments

Do Not Be Afraid

Take and Eat

Pray without Ceasing

Take Up Your Cross

ABOUT THE AUTHOR

Jared Dees is the creator of TheReligionTeacher.com, a popular website that provides practical resources and teaching strategies to religious educators. A respected graduate of the Alliance for Catholic Education (ACE) program at the University of Notre Dame, Dees holds master's degrees in education and theology, both from Notre Dame. He frequently gives keynotes and leads workshops at conferences, church events, and school in-services throughout the year on a variety of topics. He lives near South Bend, Indiana, with his wife and children.

Learn more about Jared's books, speaking events, and other projects at jareddees.com.

Made in the USA
Middletown, DE
27 November 2020